CELEBRATING THE FAMILY NAME OF LEE

Celebrating the Family Name of Lee

Walter the Educator

Silent King Books
a WhichHead Entertainment Imprint

Copyright © 2024 by Walter the Educator

All rights reserved. No part of this book may be reproduced in any manner whatsoever without written permission except in the case of brief quotations embodied in critical articles and reviews.

First Printing, 2024

Disclaimer

This book is a literary work; the story is not about specific persons, locations, situations, and/or circumstances unless mentioned in a historical context. Any resemblance to real persons, locations, situations, and/or circumstances is coincidental. This book is for entertainment and informational purposes only. The author and publisher offer this information without warranties expressed or implied. No matter the grounds, neither the author nor the publisher will be accountable for any losses, injuries, or other damages caused by the reader's use of this book. The use of this book acknowledges an understanding and acceptance of this disclaimer.

Celebrating the Family Name of Lee is a memory book that belongs to the Celebrating Family Name Book Series by Walter the Educator. Collect them all and more books at WaltertheEducator.com

USE THE EXTRA SPACE TO DOCUMENT YOUR FAMILY MEMORIES THROUGHOUT THE YEARS

LEE

From the seed of ancient roots, where history sings,
Celebrating the Family Name of

Lee

The name Lee echoes, like wind through wings,

In fields of time, where generations sow,

A name carved in stone, where rivers flow.

Through valleys deep and mountains high,

The Lees have soared, touched the sky,

A lineage strong, woven tight,

In the tapestry of life, shining bright.

Each Lee a leaf on a mighty tree,

Bound by the roots of eternity,

Branches reaching to the sun,

In the forest of the world, they are one.

Whispers of wisdom in the Lee blood run,

A legacy passed from father to son,

From mother to daughter, a sacred thread,

Through the ages, a path they've tread.
Celebrating the Family Name of

Lee

The Lees are warriors, gentle and bold,

Guardians of stories yet untold,

With hearts of courage, spirits free,

They stand as pillars, strong as can be.

In every step, a rhythm of grace,

In every glance, a familiar face,

The Lees are more than just a name,

They are a flame, an eternal flame.

Through the storms of life, they never sway,

With each generation, they find their way,

From ancient lands to shores anew,

The name Lee remains steadfast and true.

They've walked with kings, yet kept their heart,

In every Lee, a work of art,

Crafted by time, polished by care,
Celebrating the Family Name of

In the world's great canvas, they are rare.

Each Lee a story, each Lee a song,

In the grand parade of life, they belong,

With pride they carry the torch of old,

In their veins, a tale of gold.

For the Lees are not just of flesh and bone,

But of spirit, heart, and soul alone,

In their name, a legacy stands,
Celebrating the Family Name of

A family united, hand in hand.

ABOUT THE CREATOR

Walter the Educator is one of the pseudonyms for Walter Anderson. Formally educated in Chemistry, Business, and Education, he is an educator, an author, a diverse entrepreneur, and he is the son of a disabled war veteran. "Walter the Educator" shares his time between educating and creating. He holds interests and owns several creative projects that entertain, enlighten, enhance, and educate, hoping to inspire and motivate you. Follow, find new works, and stay up to date with Walter the Educator™

at WaltertheEducator.com

www.ingramcontent.com/pod-product-compliance
Lightning Source LLC
LaVergne TN
LVHW012051070526
838201LV00082B/3914